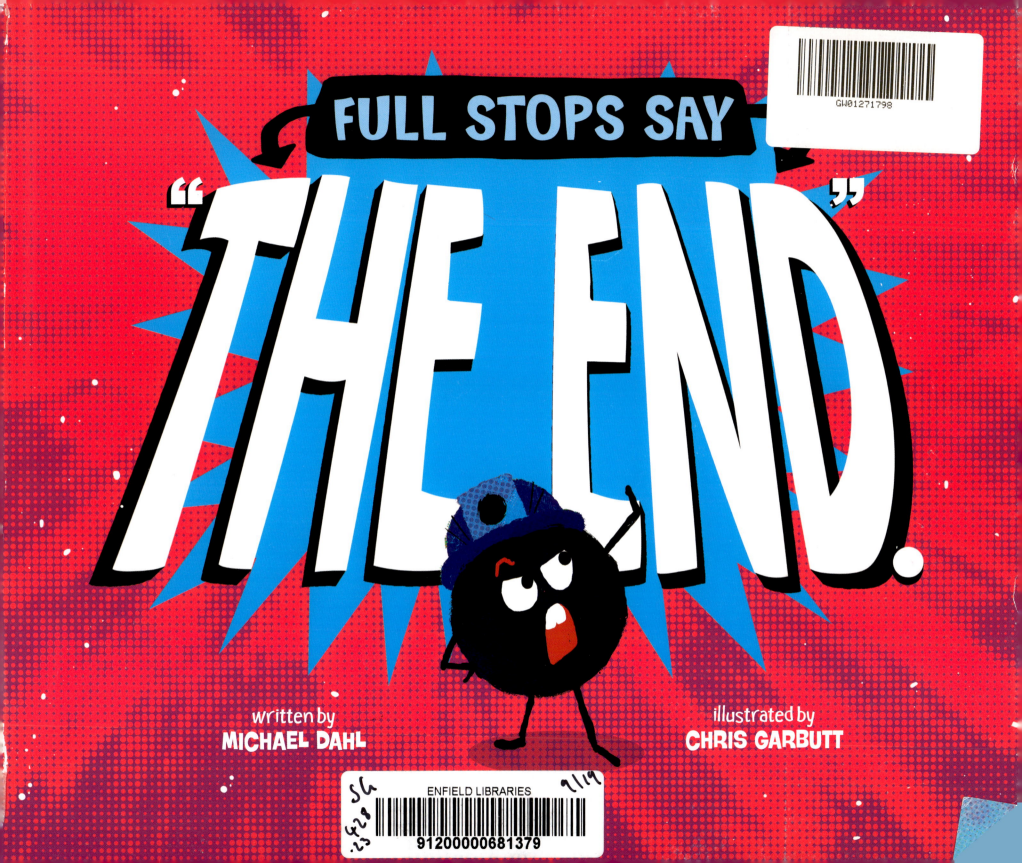

London Borough of Enfield	
91200000681379	
Askews & Holts	Aug-2019
428.23 JUNIOR NON-FI	£7.99

A full stop is **BUSY**.

A full stop does not mess around.

Full stops pop up at the **END** of sentences.

The wind howled. Trees shook and shadows danced. The moon hid behind heavy clouds.

- Like me!
- Me too!
- And me!

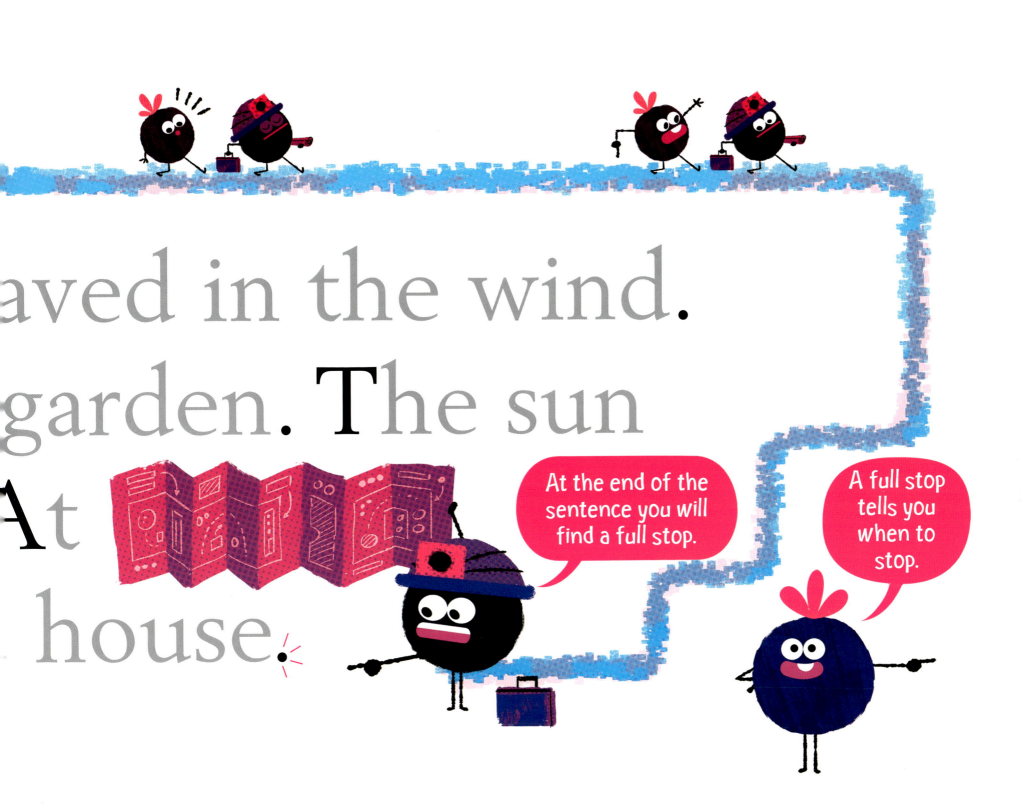

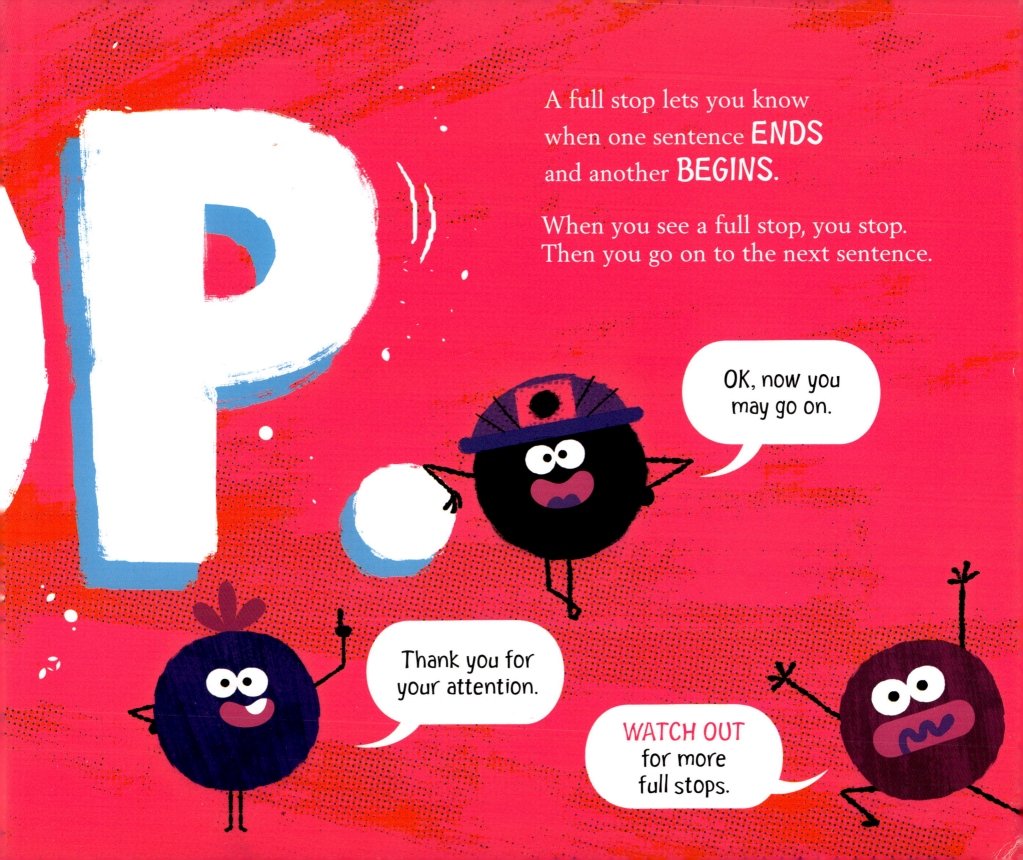

Without full stops, sentences would look like this.

princess heard a sound and dragon belched flames at the cess cried out the wild boy of it caught on fire the dragon ess hung the creatur

the creature's terrible bat-like wings
the wild boy was blown back by th

You can also find a full stop at the end of an abbreviation. An abbreviation is a shorter way of writing a long word.

"This is really helpful if you are squeezed for space."

JAN.	FEBRUARY	MARCH	APRIL
MAY	JUNE	JULY	AUGUST
SEPTEMBER	OCTOBER	NOVEMBER	DECEMBER

UARY

"Here are more full stops. Just in time."

Abbr.

Full stops can do **LOTS OF JOBS.**

There are so many other jobs, we can't even squeeze them all into this book.

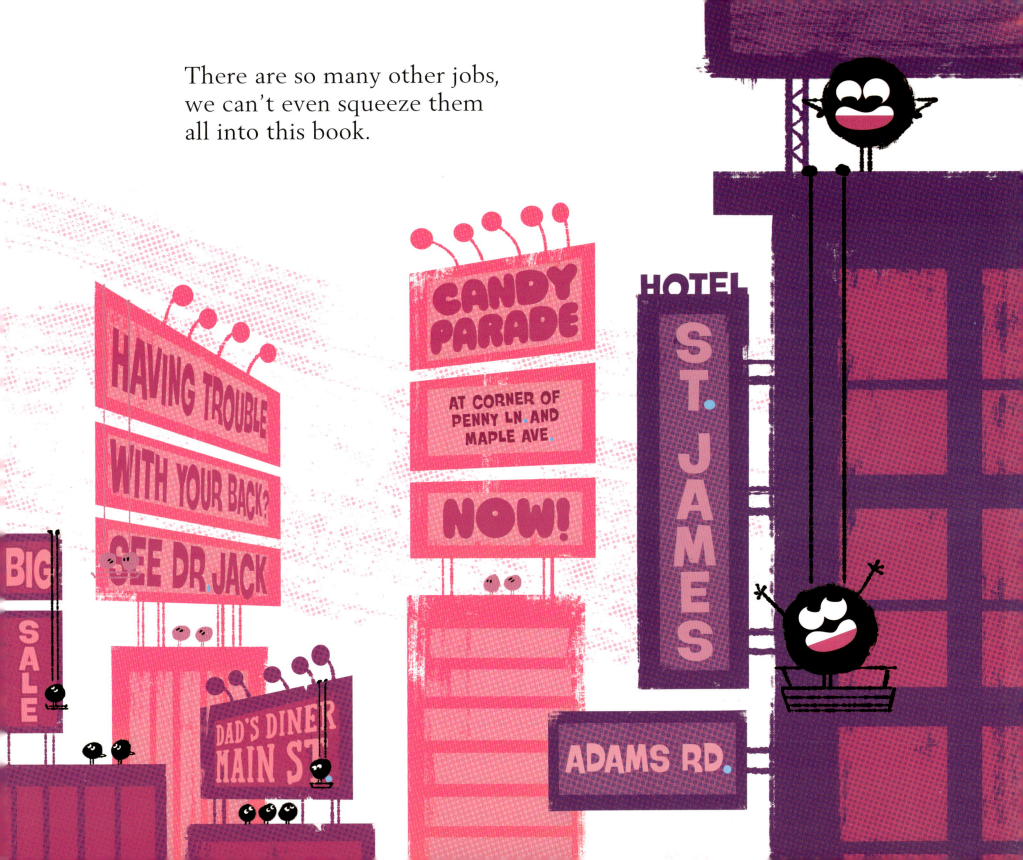

POINTS ABOUT

Full stops are found at the end of **STATEMENTS**.
The sentences here make a statement.

The wind howled.

The shadows danced.

Sometimes full stops are used at the end of **COMMAND SENTENCES**.
These sentences tell you to do something.

Watch out for more full stops.

Full stops are often used in **ABBREVIATIONS**.
They help us shorten words.

You can use Oct. to stand for October.

FULL STOPS

A full stop can come after a person's title but before his or her name.

Dr. Mason looks for full stops in her paper.

To shorten a person's name, we can use his or her initials. We can place a full stop after an initial.

R.J. signed his initials on the document.

We can also use full stops to help us tell the time.

At 10 a.m. the bell will ring for playtime.

ABOUT THE AUTHOR

Michael Dahl is the author of more than 200 books for children and has won the AEP Distinguished Achievement Award three times for his non-fiction. He is the author of the bestselling *Bedtime for Batman* and *You're A Star, Wonder Woman!* picture books. He has written dozens of books of jokes, riddles and puns. He likes to play with words. At school, he read the dictionary for fun. Really. And his favourite words are adverbs (*really* is an adverb, by the way).

ABOUT THE ILLUSTRATOR

Chris Garbutt hails from a family of tea-drinking hedgehogs that live deep in the magical hills of Yorkshire. He has spent most of his time on this planet drawing cartoons and comics in London, Paris and, most recently, Los Angeles, where he now creates funny pictures in exchange for cake. Most recently he has been the executive producer, show-runner and art director of a TV series he co-created at Nickelodeon called *Pinky Malinky*, available on Netflix.

GLOSSARY

abbreviation a shortened version of a word

capital letter a larger version of a letter; used at the beginning of a sentence or as the first letter in a proper name

declarative sentence a sentence that makes a statement

imperative sentence a sentence that gives a command

initial a letter that stands for a person's name

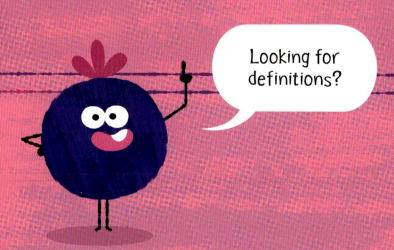

Looking for definitions?

FIND OUT MORE

First Illustrated Grammar and Punctuation (Illustrated Dictionary), Jane Bingham (Usborne, 2019)

Oxford Primary Grammar and Punctuation Flashcards (OUP, 2015)

Visual Guide to Grammar and Punctuation: First Reference for Young Writers and Readers (DK, 2017)

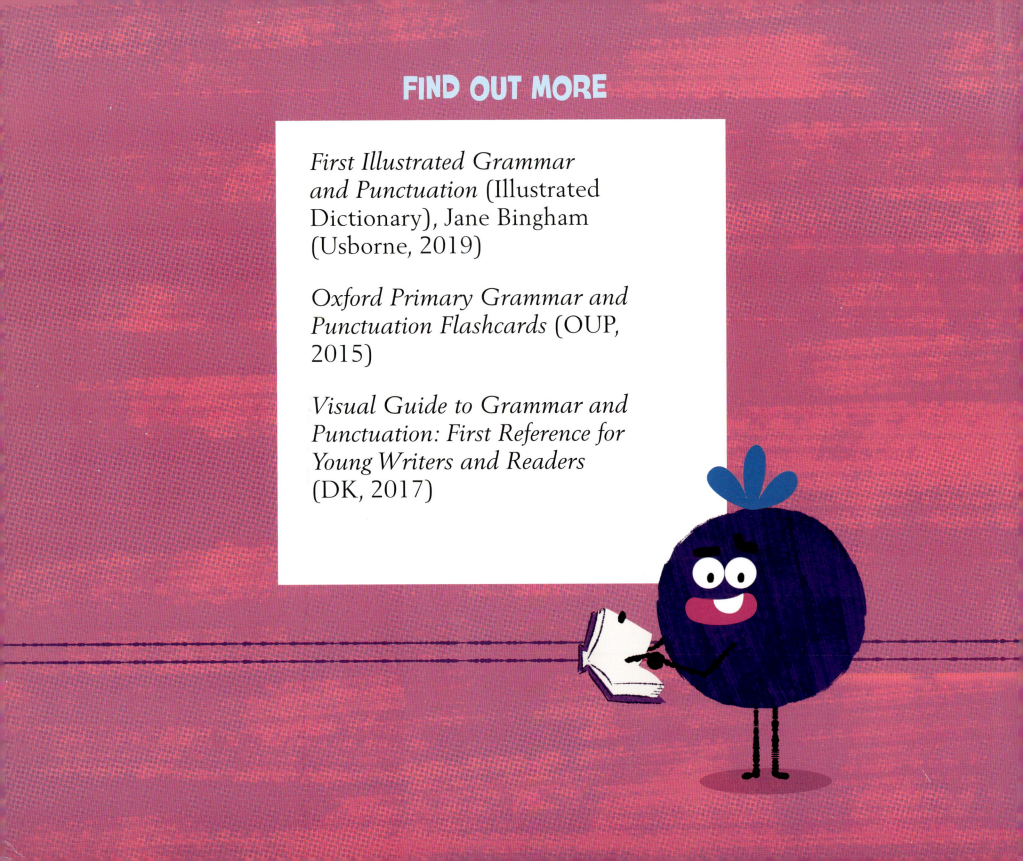

COMPREHENSION QUESTIONS

1. What is a statement sentence? Give an example.

2. What kind of sentence tells someone to do something? Give an example.

3. What titles can be abbreviated? List three examples.

WEBSITES AND APPS

Find some fun games for practising punctuation here:
www.funenglishgames.com/grammargames/punctuation.html

Check out the **Squeebles Punctuation App** for fun activities to help you practise your skills!

OTHER TITLES IN THE SERIES

Commas Say "Take a Break"
Exclamation Marks Say "Wow!"
Question Marks Say "What?"

Raintree is an imprint of Capstone Global Library Limited, a company incorporated in England and Wales having its registered office at 264 Banbury Road, Oxford, OX2 7DY – Registered company number: 6695582

www.raintree.co.uk
myorders@raintree.co.uk

Text © Capstone Global Library Limited 2020

All rights reserved. No part of this publication may be reproduced in any form or by any means (including photocopying or storing it in any medium by electronic means and whether or not transiently or incidentally to some other use of this publication) without the written permission of the copyright owner, except in accordance with the provisions of the Copyright, Designs and Patents Act 1988 or under the terms of a licence issued by the Copyright Licensing Agency, Barnard's Inn, 86 Fetter Lane, London, EC4A 1EN (www.cla.co.uk). Applications for the copyright owner's written permission should be addressed to the publisher.

Editor: Shelly Lyons
Designers: Aruna Rangarajan and Hilary Wacholz
Creative Director: Nathan Gassman
Production Specialist: Katy LaVigne
The illustrations in this book were created digitally.
Printed and bound in India

ISBN 978 1 4747 7185 6

British Library Cataloguing in Publication Data:
A full catalogue record for this book is available from the British Library.